Panayiotis Kalorkoti: The Artist as Collector

Panayiotis Kalorkoti's early reputation is largely based on his inventive and particular use of colour etching. Employing a collage approach (which he calls 'a play of the mind') to the layout and structuring of serial images, these impressive prints combine elements of photomontage with grids like a comic strip. Although he began as a painter, Kalorkoti was dissatisfied with his work in that medium, judging it to be literally too unwieldy and heavy for what he had to say. So he developed his layered multi-plate approach to print-making, which in sheer density (of content as well as technique) can be said to rival oil painting when operating as satiric commentary in the tradition of Goya, Hogarth, Daumier, Dix and Grosz. Only in 1994 did Kalorkoti once again return to painting, with a series of woodblock-like acrylics done during a residency in Grizedale Forest. He now works mostly on paper, in acrylic and watercolour, but hasn't used oil for 16 years. The body of work under discussion here, which depicts semi-anonymous assemblies of schematized natural forms, takes watercolour to new heights of decorative and emblematic meaning.

Art for Kalorkoti is a kind of questioning, of essences and of appearances, to which there are no easy or definitive answers. ('There is no one truth', he says.) In other words, art acts as a species of philosophical enquiry, engaging with the mundanity of life, through an investigation of visual languages. Refreshingly in this ego-dominated age, Kalorkoti is more interested in raising issues than in projecting himself, though there remains a didactic impulse behind his work. He cannot resist drawing our attention to specific topics which have an underlying political content (in the widest sense). He deplores romanticism, but neither is he a 'doom merchant'; thankfully, a sense of humour preserves his sense of proportion.

Kalorkoti is a compulsive collector - not only of information but of faces, drawn or photographed, sometimes reduced to masks or pictograms, and now of schematized forms from nature. We collect to make sense of the world around us, possibly to convince ourselves we have tamed it. Kalorkoti's line portraits have a laconic power: drawing at its most economically descriptive. Is it in the service of identifying types or individuals? There's a dispassionate purity to his gaze, not unlike the portrait drawings of John Craxton. Craxton, who has made his home in Greece for many years, is much influenced by Byzantine art. Kalorkoti, born and brought up in Cyprus (he didn't come to

England until he was nearly nine), is the natural heir of Cypriot Greek and Byzantine icon painting.

It has long been Kalorkoti's practise to make quick sketches - often in their hundreds - for a new project, an activity which for him is rather like doodling. These sketches do not relate directly to the paintings which follow, but are a form of limbering up, of discovering and testing the boundaries of a subject. Kalorkoti also takes a great many photographs by way of research, though it is revealing that he doesn't tend to use newspaper photos - though the appearance of his printed work might suggest it.

Kalorkoti has very specific ideas about the portrayal of human beings. The people he draws so obsessively - and a series of his portrait drawings might extend to 225, as the Gateshead Garden Festival group does - are the ordinary people he encounters in the course of his daily round. For, he asks, why should we only be interested in portraits of famous people? According to Kalorkoti, the modern period is intimately involved with anonymity. *Anyone* will make a good subject, though not necessarily an interesting one to others. At the base of all portraiture is the difficulty of really knowing another person, and of making a useful statement about them with any degree of accuracy. Kalorkoti dismisses the fashionable iargon about the psychological penetration of modern portraiture - he's content if a good image results. To this end, in his watercolours, he might dissolve the features, into and out of representation, from negative to positive, within a whole variety of painterly endings and beginnings.

Kalorkoti has made watercolour portraits in the past (there are groups of them dated 1994 and 1997, for instance), but they are not among his most successful or convincing representations of people. There is a graphic coarseness or unsubtlety to them which seems at odds with the delicacy of the medium. A 1995 group of watercolours entitled *Reflect* consist of broken-down blobby images of faces in close-up, which mimic the distortions of newspaper reproductions of photographs. As do the series of *Group* and *Situation* heads from 1996.

In 1994 he made a series of 24 rather more abstract watercolour figures, in order to re-acquaint himself with the strengths and weaknesses of the medium. They are elemental in their treatment of light and colour, full of

PANAYIOTIS KALORKOTI

Flowers

in

Watercolour

gallery k

LONDON
101-103 Heath Street, Hampstead London NW3 6SS
Tel: + 44 (0)20 7794 4949 - Fax: + 44 (0)20 7431 4833
Internet:www.gallery-k.co.uk   E-mail:art@gallery- k.co.uk

NICOSIA
14 Evrou Street, Strovolos, 2003, Nicosia, Cyprus
Tel: +357 0)2 341123 Fax: +357 (0)2 341124
E-mail:galleryk@cytanet.com.cy

Published for the exhibition,
Panayiotis Kalorkoti, Flowers in Watercolour
Held at Gallery K, London, from 29 April - 27 May 2001
and Gallery K, Nicosia, from 1 October - 30 October 2001

ISBN 1 898710 38 4

Cover: Two Forms 4
Back Cover: Flowers 4 *(Detail)*
Page 40: Auriculas 4 *(Detail)*

dissolving figures - the body as fire and spirit, shimmering and re-configuring on the page. Again in 1999 he painted several large watercolours of a figure in movement, a dancing torso on a predominantly yellow or red ground, which had the effect of eroding the figure. The issue of individual identity, alluded to here, is re-presented under another guise in his most recent body of work - 48 luminous watercolours of flowers and insects.

At first sight, these new images look like the colour plates from *The Observer's Book of Insects* or *Wild Flowers*. They resemble scientific specimens (Kalorkoti considered following a career in science before he opted to study art at Newcastle University and the Royal College), arranged in family groupings. The insects don't touch, and are laid out as if on cork slabs, separately, transfixed by the collector's pins. (Equally, none of the flowers overlap, as they would in real life, in a garden or vase.) Alternatively, these images resemble the brightly-coloured learning-aid illustrations to children's alphabet books - except that these collections of similar flowers and insects would prove more confusing than elucidating.

Interestingly, Kalorkoti's current explorations of watercolour again use the medium against the grain of the technique, except as found in such sub-genres as botanical illustration. There is little veiling or transparency to Kalorkoti's handling. The colour is opaque and flatly applied, almost deadpan. Typically, Kalorkoti subverts the genre as well as the technique. This is botanical illustration with a difference.

Some of the issues suggested by this body of work include strategies of survival: The concepts of camouflage - how to be safe in an increasingly dangerous world - and display: how to attract or repel, also for reasons of survival. Yet because his work is not based on scrupulous observation and recorded fact, but is often invented, the images are drained of the specific meaning of the naturalist. Art supervenes. The intense non-naturalistic colour of these new works seems to point to Kalorkoti's Mediterranean inheritance. Also perhaps to the example of teachers. He vividly remembers a day spent as a student with Patrick Heron. The purity and strength of his colour now recalls Heron and his idol Matisse, as it does Ken Kiff, another master colourist, whom Kalorkoti knew at the Royal College.

These new works are not strictly portraits of flowers or insects, for Kalorkoti doesn't want to emphasize specifics. In fact, the least successful are the most descriptive or recognizable. Narrative in these pictures is almost totally absent, to be replaced by rhythm and colour. The spatial setting is indefinite, but suggestive. A tapestry-like background layer provides movement to offset the single forms repeated in wave patterns (like synchronized swimming), with variations of explosive colour. Colour and shape create movement, and aim at universality. Kalorkoti favours autumnal tints - reds and yellows. Although the body shapes of the wasps and bees and butterflies do originate in reference books, they are adapted to the artist's aesthetic requirements. Kalorkoti doesn't work from live specimens; as he says, he is not really a nature person, but a city dweller. Like Mondrian, he dislikes green, but has introduced it into these new paintings (almost under duress) as being aesthetically necessary. Blue is an acceptable variant, but it is really red and yellow, one taking a foreground the other a background role, that Kalorkoti prefers, with the colours used as purely as possible.

Remark the precision of the drawing of these elements, it is deliberately characterless. The hard edges against the mottled grounds could be cogs as much as flowers. These flowers are geometricized, simplified, with none of the fragility of real flowers - Kalorkoti is not interested in that. Much more ordered and orderly than nature, these blossoms and insects float above their dappled backgrounds, creating the illusion of collage. Kalorkoti doesn't want to unify the surface event with the ground - he intends these different visual elements to bounce off one another. He likes the interplay of jagged fronds with smooth areas of flat colour.

Kalorkoti aims at disguising the individual insect or flower and enveloping it in a larger pattern - as we as individual units should be merely a part of the larger pattern of the universe. The more disguised the individual traits, the more successful Kalorkoti deems the picture. When the flowers look like butterflies, the eye is deceived and the pattern emerges more strongly. At times these objects could easily be other things - star loaves or rolls, Viennese whirls, fairy cakes or butterfly pasta. Here Kalorkoti engages with the Pop Art repeat imagery of Wayne Thiebaud or Warhol, and echoes its mass market presentation.

The underlying grid structure holds the elements centred in suspension - neither aligned to left or right, top or bottom. The big single blooms are all-enveloping and extend right to the edges of the paper. Paradoxically, Kalorkoti relishes petal or wing divisions. For him, these discontinuities are important, for the images should not appear too symmetrical and perfect. Likewise, the textures should be varied, but only as much as is absolutely necessary. These images are very much variations on a theme, though beguiling in their repetitions. Means are deliberately restricted, but made to speak as eloquently as chamber music. This is richness through simplicity. As Kalorkoti himself says 'I do believe that clarity of thought in the work is important'. The idea is crucial, but here is a conceptual artist who actually likes traditionally-made imagery.

What do the flowers signify? The schematized petal face assumes abstract shapes: one orange flower-head has all the dynamic tension of a kite. Elsewhere a corrugated edge against a billowy one sets up a purely abstract visual frisson. The earlier works tends to be less lyrical. A 1994 quartet of images is like a ribbon bow of articulated form - five petals which become like insect wings and then geometric and rounded. These images may look as if made with a stencil or template, but they are all individually hand-drawn. In fact, they are really hand-*painted*, for only part of the pattern is drawn out in pencil beforehand: Kalorkoti doesn't want too much pre-mapping.

The latest work, though not obviously continuing his complex dialogue with mechanical reproduction, is in fact involved just as deeply with what the reproduction of images means to us as communication. As always with Kalorkoti, burning questions are at once raised - what kind of information is provided? What degree of commentary? Surely we are dealing here with issues of repetition and individuation, of anonymity versus particularization? But why does Kalorkoti want us to spend time with these pictures? Do they contain an autobiographical sub-text?

Other commentators have read ambiguity, desolation and despair into Kalorkoti's images. There is perhaps a degree of unease and anxiety to his figure compositions, but these negative values should not be over-stressed. It is in the nature of satire to *ridicule* vices and follies, not to espouse them. Kalorkoti is too wary and knowing a commentator to indulge in cosmic despair; cosmic laughter is perhaps more in his line. The vivid monumentality of these flower and insect ballets is nothing less than life-enhancing. It is as if with his methodic arrangements and inventories, his careful division of the picture surface, and his quasi-taxonomical questing, Kalorkoti casts a shaft of light into our muddled consciousness. Once again we are assured of the fundamental interconnectedness of all things.

In the end, it's all a matter of presentation. The artist must develop an awareness of history ('for me history is not clear', comments Kalorkoti, 'where's the truth?'), for only through constant reinterpretations have we any chance of a fresh understanding. Kalorkoti tirelessly returns to an idea to probe it further, and has developed the good Modernist habit of taking things to a logical conclusion, by way of thorough serial exploration. Panayiotis Kalorkoti aims to question and challenge our assumptions, to keep us on the *qui vive*, and heighten our awareness of our relationship to the world. In this striking and provocative series of watercolours, he triumphantly achieves just that.

Andrew Lambirth   London: March 2001

1. **Form 1** 1997 Watercolour 57.5 x 76.5cm (22⁵⁄₈ x 30¹⁄₈in)

2. **Form 2** 1997 Watercolour 57.5 x 76.5cm (22⁵⁄₈ x 30¹⁄₈in)

3. **Form 3** 1997 Watercolour 57.5 x 76.5cm (22⁵/₈ x 30¹/₈in)

4. **Form 4** 1997 Watercolour 57.5 x 76.5cm (22⁵/₈ x 30¹/₈in)

5. **Form 4** *(Detail)*

6. **Scented 1** 1997 Watercolour 57.5 x 76.5cm (22⅝ x 30⅛in)

7. **Scented 2** 1997 Watercolour 57.5 x 76.5cm (22⅝ x 30⅛in)

8. **Scented 3** 1997   Watercolour 57.5 x 76.5cm (22⁵/₈ x 30¹/₈in)

9. **Scented 4** 1997   Watercolour 57.5 x 76.5cm (22⁵/₈ x 30¹/₈in)

10.
Single Form 1 1997
Watercolour
76.5 x 57.5cm (30$^{1}/_{8}$ x 22$^{5}/_{8}$in)

11.
Single Form 2 1997
Watercolour
76.5 x 57.5cm (30$^{1}/_{8}$ x 22$^{5}/_{8}$in)

12.
Single Form 3 1997
Watercolour
76.5 x 57.5cm (30$^{1}/_{8}$ x 22$^{5}/_{8}$in)

13.
Single Form 4 1997
Watercolour
76.5 x 57.5cm (30$^{1}/_{8}$ x 22$^{5}/_{8}$in)

14. **Single Form 2** (Detail)

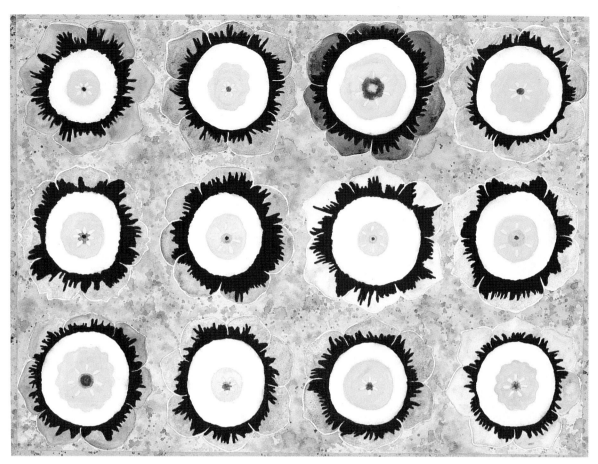

15. **Auriculas 1** 1998 Watercolour 57.5 x 76.2cm (22⁵/₈ x 30in)

16. **Auriculas 2** 1998 Watercolour 57.5 x 76.2cm (22⁵/₈ x 30in)

17. **Auriculas 3** 1998 Watercolour 57.5 x 76.2cm (22⁵/₈ x 30in)

18. **Auriculas 4** 1998 Watercolour 57.5 x 76.2cm (22⁵/₈ x 30in)

19. **Species 1** 1998 Watercolour 57.5 x 76.2cm (22⅝ x 30in)

20. **Species 2** 1998 Watercolour 57.5 x 76.2cm (22⅝ x 30in)

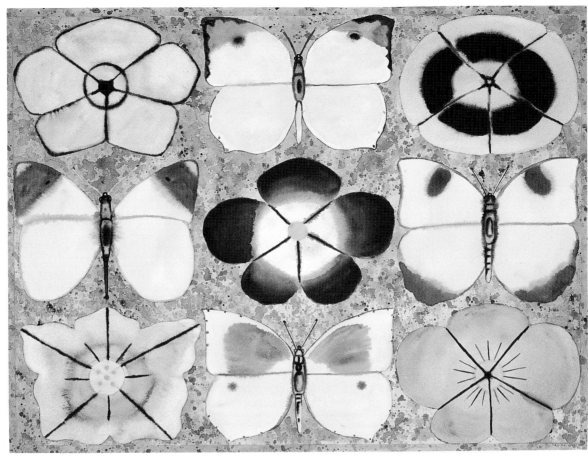

21. **Species 3** 1998 Watercolour 57.5 x 76.2cm (22⁵/₈ x 30in)

22. **Species 4** 1998 Watercolour 57.5 x 76.2cm (22⁵/₈ x 30in)

23. **Butterflies 1** 1998 Watercolour 57.5 x 76.2cm (22⁵/₈ x 30in)

24. **Butterflies 2** 1998 Watercolour 57.5 x 75.9cm (22⁵/₈ x 29⁷/₈in)

25. **Butterflies 3** 1998 Watercolour 57.5 x 75.9cm (22⁵/₈ x 29⁷/₈in)

26. **Butterflies 4** 1998 Watercolour 57.5 x 75.9cm (22⁵/₈ x 29⁷/₈in)

27. **Individual Forms 1** 1999 Watercolour 57.1 x 76.9cm (22$\frac{1}{2}$ x 30$\frac{1}{4}$in)

28. **Individual Forms 2** 1999 Watercolour 57.1 x 76.9cm (22$\frac{1}{2}$ x 30$\frac{1}{4}$in)

29. **Individual Forms 3** 1999 Watercolour 57.1 x 76.9cm (22¹/₂ x 30¹/₄in)

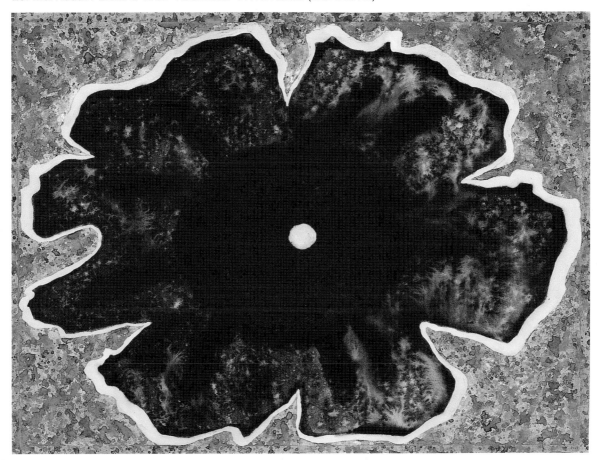

30. **Individual Forms 4** 1999 Watercolour 57.1 x 76.9cm (22¹/₂ x 30¹/₄in)

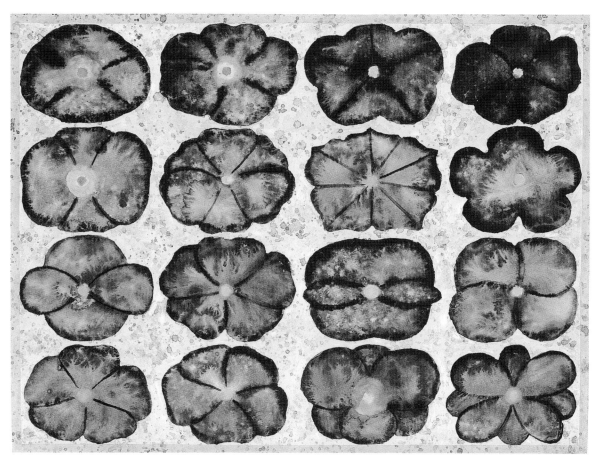

31. **Variety 1** 1999 Watercolour 57.1 x 76.9cm (22$\frac{1}{2}$ x 30$\frac{1}{4}$in)

32. **Variety 2** 1999 Watercolour 57.5 x 76.9cm (22$\frac{5}{8}$ x 30$\frac{1}{4}$in)

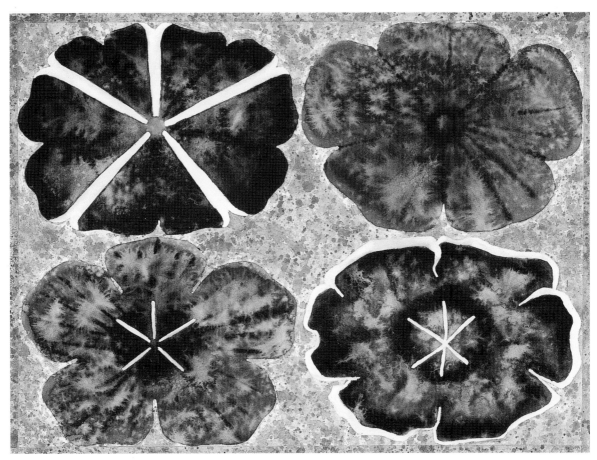

33. **Variety 3** 1999 Watercolour 57.5 x 76.9cm (22⅝ x 30¼in)

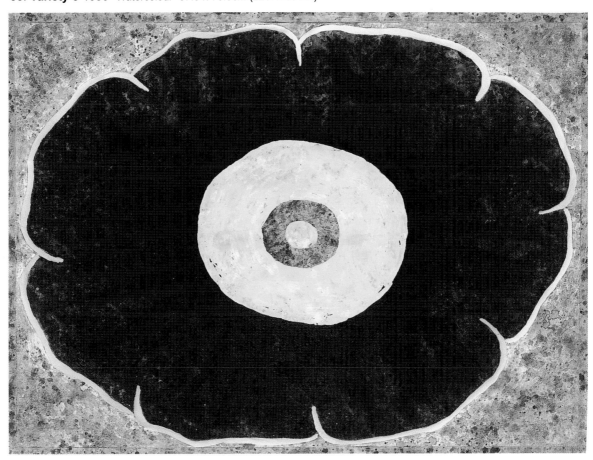

34. **Variety 4** 1999 Watercolour 57.5 x 76.9cm (22⅝ x 30¼in)

35. **Scent 1** 2000 Watercolour 57.5 x 76.5cm (22⅝ x 30⅛in)

36. **Scent 2** 2000 Watercolour 57.5 x 76.5cm (22⅝ x 30⅛in)

37. **Scent 3** 2000 Watercolour 57.5 x 76.5cm (22⁵/₈ x 30¹/₈in)

38. **Scent 4** 2000 Watercolour 57.5 x 76.5cm (22⁵/₈ x 30¹/₈in)

39. **Flowers 1** 2000 Watercolour 57.5 x 76.5cm (22⁵/₈ x 30¹/₈in)

40. **Flowers 2** 2000 Watercolour 57.5 x 76.2cm (22⁵/₈ x 30in)

41. **Flowers 3** 2000 Watercolour 57.5 x 76.5cm (22⅝ x 30⅛in)

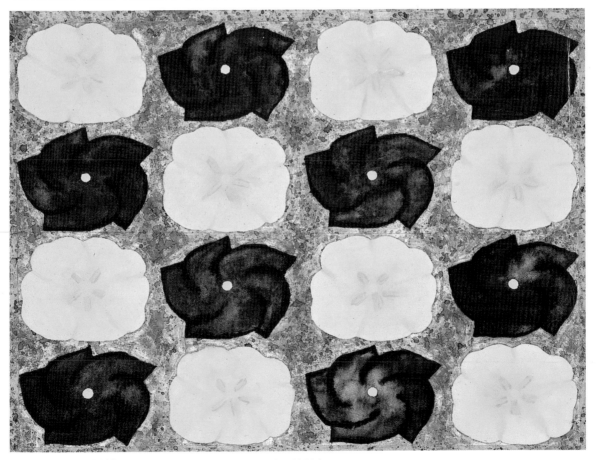

42. **Flowers 4** 2000 Watercolour 57.5 x 76.5cm (22⅝ x 30⅛in)

43.
Variation 1 2001
Watercolour
76.5 x 56.9cm (30^1/$_8$ x 22^3/$_8$in)

44.
Variation 2 2001
Watercolour
76.5 x 56.9cm (30^1/$_8$ x 22^3/$_8$in)

45.
Variation 3 2001
Watercolour
76.5 x 56.9cm (30^1/$_8$ x 22^3/$_8$in)

46.
Variation 4 2001
Watercolour
76.5 x 56.9cm (30^1/$_8$ x 22^3/$_8$in)

47. **Variation 4** *(Detail)*

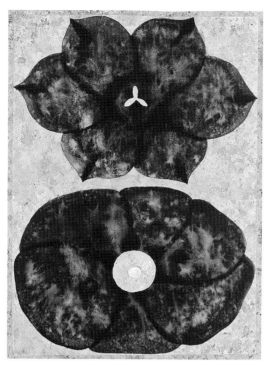

48.
Two Forms 1 2001
Watercolour
76.5 x 56.9cm (30¹/₈ x 22³/₈in)

49.
Two Forms 2 2001
Watercolour
76.5 x 56.9cm (30¹/₈ x 22³/₈in)

50.
Two Forms 3 2001
Watercolour
76.5 x 56.9cm (30¹/₈ x 22³/₈in)

51.
Two Forms 4 2001
Watercolour
76.5 x 56.9cm (30¹/₈ x 22³/₈in)

52. **Two Forms 4** *(Detail)*

53. **Sketch 1** 1997 Pencil on paper 14.8 x 20.3cm (5¹³/₁₆ x 8in)

54. **Sketch 2** 1997 Pencil on paper 14.8 x 20.3cm (5¹³/₁₆ x 8in)

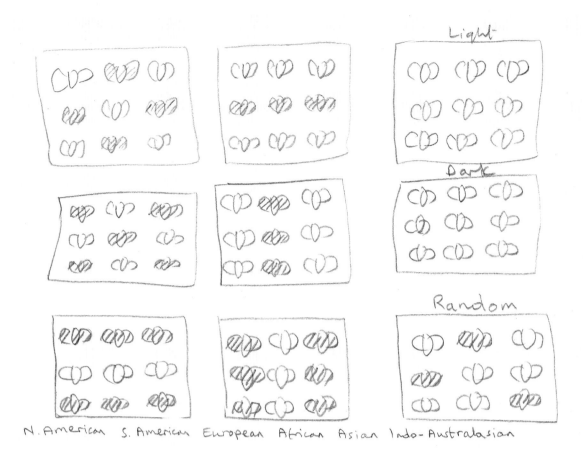

Light

Dark

Random

N. American   S. American   European   African   Asian   Indo-Australasian

55. **Sketch 3** 1997 Pencil on paper 14.8 x 20.3cm (5¹³/₁₆ x 8in)

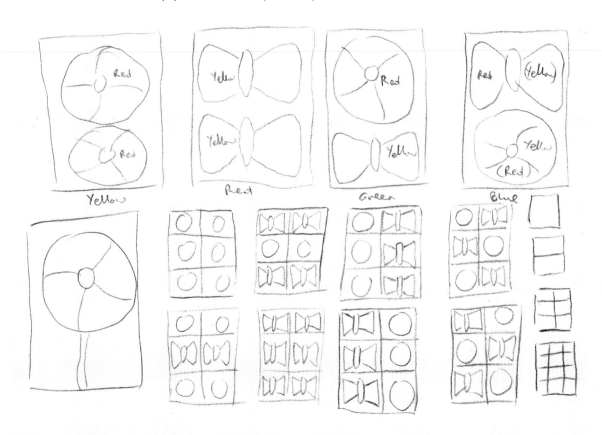

56. **Sketch 4** 2000 Pencil on paper 14.8 x 20.3cm (5¹³/₁₆ x 8in)

Biography

1957   Born in Ayios Amvrossios, Cyprus

1976-80   Newcastle upon Tyne University, B.A. (Hons.) 1st Class in Fine Art

1982-85   Royal College of Art, London, M.A. in Fine Art

1985   Artist in Residence, Leeds Playhouse

1986-87   Koninklijke Akademie voor Kunst en Vormgeving, 's-Hertogenbosch
              (Netherlands Government Scholarship)

1988   Bartlett Fellow in the Visual Arts (Newcastle upon Tyne University)
              Commissioned by the Imperial War Museum, London; People's Theatre, Newcastle

1989   Commissioned by the Borough of Darlington; Borough of Hartlepool;
              The Grizedale Society (also commissioned in 1991 and 1992)

1989-90   Commissioned by the National Garden Festival, Gateshead

1992   Artist in Residence, Cleveland

1994   Artist in Residence, The Grizedale Society

              Taught part-time and visiting lecturer at a number of Art Colleges

Public Collections

Stedelijk Museum, Amsterdam
British Council, London
Imperial War Museum, London
Laing Art Gallery, Newcastle
University of Northumbria at Newcastle
Edinburgh University
Hatton Gallery, Newcastle University
Gray Art Gallery and Museum, Hartlepool
Shipley Art Gallery, Gateshead
Darlington Arts Centre
Cleveland Gallery, Middlesbrough
Gallery in the Forest, Grizedale
Northern Arts
Rank
Xerox
IBM

List of catalogues published:-

1988 *Kalorkoti,* Hatton Gallery, Newcastle upon Tyne and Tour (catalogue-text by Eva Krabbe, 68 pages with 64 illustrations, 16 in colour)

1990 *A Retrospective of Etchings and Screenprints 1978-89,* Imperial War Museum, London (catalogue-text by Frank Whitford, 40 pages with 33 illustrations, 20 in colour)

1990 *National Garden Festival Commission, 1990,* Gateshead and Tour (catalogue-text by Roger Wollen, 40 pages with 234 illustrations, 8 in colour)

1992 *A Retrospective View 1985-91,* Design Works, Gateshead (catalogue-text by Timothy Hyman, 32 pages with 46 illustrations, 44 in colour)

1992 *Etchings and Drawings,* Cleveland Gallery, Middlesbrough and Tour (catalogue-text by Frank Van den Broeck, 72 pages with 93 illustrations, 48 in colour)

1994 *Retrospective (Etchings 1983-93),* Gallery K, London and Tour (catalogue-text by Roger Cardinal, 32 pages with 44 illustrations, 33 in colour)

1995 *Reflections of Grizedale (Acrylics, Watercolours, Etchings),* Gallery in the Forest, Grizedale (catalogue-text by Edward Lucie-Smith, 60 pages with 43 illustrations, 36 in colour)

1997 *An Exhibition of Acrylics, Watercolours and Etchings,* Design Works, Gateshead (catalogue-text by Mel Gooding, 60 pages with 55 illustrations, 53 in colour)

1998 *Heads, Faces and Figures,* Shipley Art Gallery, Gateshead and Tour (catalogue-text by Robin Gibson, 40 pages with 70 illustrations, 53 in colour)

2000 *Acrylics, Watercolours and Etchings,* AdHoc Gallery, Buddle Arts Centre, North Tyneside, (catalogue-text by Norbert Lynton, 40 pages with 44 illustrations, 43 in colour)

2001 *Flowers in Watercolour,* Gallery K, London and Tour (Catalogue-text by Andrew Lambirth, 40 pages with 57 illustrations, 51 in colour)

List of pamphlets published:-

1998 Artists Series (text by Panayiotis Kalorkoti, 8 pages with 8 illustrations)

1990 Works in the Imperial War Museum Collection (text by Angela Weight, 8 pages with 7 illustrations, 4 in colour)

Selected Exhibitions

Solo Exhibitions

1980   Newcastle Polytechnic Gallery

1981   Bede Gallery, Jarrow
Hendersons Gallery, Edinburgh

1982   Bede Monastery Museum, Jarrow
Ceolfrith Gallery, Sunderland Arts Centre
Pentonville Gallery, London

1984   Abbot Hall Art Gallery and Museum, Kendal

1987   The Minories, Colchester
Steendrukkerij Amsterdam B.V.

1988-89   Hatton Gallery, Newcastle and tour: Darlington Arts Centre; Gray Art Gallery and Museum, Hartlepool; Queen's Hall Arts Centre, Hexham (Catalogue - text by Eva Krabbe, 68 pages with 64 illustrations, 16 in colour)

1990   Imperial War Museum, London (Catalogue - text by Frank Whitford, 40 pages with 33 illustrations, 20 in colour)
National Garden Festival, Gateshead (Catalogue - text by Roger Wollen, 40 pages with 234 illustrations, 8 in colour)

1992   Design Works, Gateshead (Catalogue - text by Timothy Hyman, 32 pages with 46 illustrations, 44 in colour)
Cleveland Gallery, Middlesbrough and tour: Steendrukkerij Amsterdam B.V. (Catalogue - text by Frank Van den Broeck, 72 pages with 93 illustrations, 48 in colour)

1994   Gallery K, London and tour: Galerie Titanium, Athens (Catalogue - text by Roger Cardinal, 32 pages with 44 illustrations, 33 in colour)

1995   Gallery in the Forest, Grizedale (Catalogue - text by Edward Lucie-Smith, 60 pages with 43 illustrations, 36 in colour)

1997   Design Works, Gateshead (Catalogue - text by Mel Gooding, 60 pages with 55 illustrations, 53 in colour)

1998-99   Shipley Art Gallery, Gateshead and tour: Herbert Art Gallery & Museum, Coventry (Catalogue - text by Robin Gibson, 40 pages with 70 illustrations, 53 in colour)

1999   AdHoc Gallery, Buddle Arts Centre, North Tyneside (Catalogue - text by Norbert Lynton, 40 pages with 44 illustrations, 43 in colour)

2001   Gallery K, London and tour: Gallery K, Nicosia (Catalogue - text by Andrew Lambirth, 40 pages with 57 illustrations, 51 in colour)

Group Exhibitions

1980   The Stone Gallery, Newcastle

1981   *Small Works* Newcastle Polytechnic Gallery

1982   *and Printmaking* Waterloo Gallery, London (Catalogue)

1983   *Stowells Trophy* Royal Academy of Arts, London
Northern Young Contemporaries (awarded Granada Prize) Whitworth Art Gallery, Manchester

1984   Bath Festival Painting Competition
New Contemporaries ICA, London (Catalogue)

1985   *Printmakers at the Royal College of Art* Concourse Gallery, Barbican Centre, London (Catalogue - text by William Feaver)
Fresh Air St. Paul's Gallery, Leeds
Whitworth Young Contemporaries Whitworth Art Gallery, Manchester

1986   *Tradition and Innovation in Printmaking Today* Milton Keynes Exhibition Gallery and tour: Ferens Art Gallery, Hull; Andrew Grant Gallery, Edinburgh; Concourse Gallery, Barbican Centre, London; Aspex Gallery, Portsmouth (Catalogue)
Between Identity and Politics, A New Art Gimpel Fils, London and tour: Darlington Arts Centre; Gimpel and Weitzenhoffer, New York (Catalogue)
Fresh Art Concourse Gallery, Barbican Centre, London (Catalogue)
Whitechapel Open Whitechapel Art Gallery, London

1987   Athena Art Awards, Concourse Gallery, Barbican Centre, London
Which Side of the Fence Imperial War Museum, London

1989   *The Artistic Records Committee: A Retrospective 1972-1989* Imperial War Museum, London

1991   *Homage to Goya* and *Soldier* Museum of Modern Art, Oxford

1993   *The Portrait Now* National Portrait Gallery, London (Catalogue - text by Robin Gibson)
Gallery K, London (Catalogue - text by Mary Rose Beaumont)

1995   *Heads and Tales II* Herbert Art Gallery & Museum, Coventry

2001   *A New Light* Peterborough Museum & Art Gallery